Letters to My Angry Self

Dr. De'Andrea Matthews

Published by:
Claire Aldin Publications
P. O. Box 453
Southfield, MI 48037

Scripture quotations marked (ESV) are taken from THE HOLY BIBLE, ENGLISH STANDARD VERSION®, Copyright© 2001 by Crossway, a publishing ministry of Good News Publishers. Used by permission.

Scripture quotations marked (CEV) are taken from the CONTEMPORARY ENGLISH VERSION, Copyright© 1995 by the American Bible Society. Used by permission.

Scripture quotations marked (NIV) are taken from THE HOLY BIBLE, NEW INTERNATIONAL VERSION®. Copyright© 1973, 1978, 1984, 2011 by Biblica, Inc.™. Used by permission of Zondervan.

Library of Congress Control Number: 2024945705

ISBN 978-1-954274-18-1 paperback
ISBN 978-1-954274-19-8 eBook

Printed in the United States of America.

LETTERS TO MY ANGRY SELF

CONTENTS

PREFACE

THE DANCE OF ANGER

Sitting on the side of the white porcelain bathtub, my head hung low as I desperately searched for answers. At this point in my life, I realized that something had to change. In the morning, I would pray and plan to have a good day. By night, I would explode in anger, spewing hurtful words that I could not take back. My most important relationships were spiraling out of control, and I had no clue how to repair the damage already done.

Anger is an emotion, which of itself isn't bad; but it is the spirit of anger that leads to trouble. Galatians 5 confirmed this, as I was reminded that outbursts of wrath are works of the flesh. I had been operating in my flesh, but pleading the blood of Jesus over everyone else. Alone and lonely, I cried out to God. In those moments of solitude, God showed me that at the root of my anger was a spirit of perfectionism. As a child, I was rewarded for perfect attendance, perfect citizenship, and perfect grades. These achievements translated into unrealistic expectations in my adult life. I expected my kids to behave perfectly, to perform in stellar ways, and to make me look like a perfect parent. Boy was I in for a surprise! My anger continued to build. I had no control over others and those within my control were rebelling. I was being forced to deal with me. As a result, I was lost and at a crossroad with God.

The following letters are stories and personal experiences that I have encountered over time. In each letter, corresponding Scripture is given to support this battle against the spirit of anger with the truth of God's Word. I encourage you to read the letters and meditate upon each corresponding Scripture. My desire is that through my transparency, you will find the necessary tools to tackle anger and win. The results are explained in the following *Letters to My Angry Self.*

CHAPTER ONE

WHAT DID I DO WRONG?

Pork chops fried to a golden brown, mashed potatoes with gravy, and green beans cooked with onions sat on the table, getting colder by the minute. Our son is nestled in bed following a nice bubble bath with his favorite bath toys. I decide to prop my feet up, watch some television, and rub my enormous belly while I waited for my husband to come home from work. Dozing off halfway between shows, I wake up to find that he is still not at home. Looking around at the clock, I blink several times to make sure that I am seeing correctly. 2:43 a.m. No sign of him, yet. The house phone hasn't rung and I dare not disturb him at his second job.

We both were young when we married; I was 20, he was 23. For the first time, I decided to join my mother in Lent. She told me I needed to give something up, so I did. I gave up chocolate, drinking and having sex. When Easter (the end of Lent) came that year, what do you think I did? I ate lots of chocolate, I went to a cabaret to celebrate being able to drink again, and I had sex. That night was memorable for all the wrong reasons.

The cabaret we went to ended tragically. One of the organizers lost his life to gunfire after trying to stop a thief who raided the coat check. My leather coat was one of the items stolen. Alcohol impairs your ability to think rationally. I had sex with my "man candy" without protection. (He thought I was still on the pill like the last time we "hooked up.") Nine months later to the date, my oldest son was born.

My boyfriend and I were not together at the time of my son's conception, but like most on again/off again relationships, we got back together. I had to not only tell my beau that I was pregnant, but he wanted to know who the father was. I was grateful that he cared, but mad that I had to disclose my indiscretions. Despite the fact that I already had a son by another man, he asked me to marry him. He actually *wanted* to marry me anyway and be a father to my child. Sounds like a happy ending, right? Far from it.

I was ready to be a wife. I had planned this my whole life. Being a wife and mother were key scenarios in my perfect dream. We got married when my son was six months old. It was a beautiful ceremony with family and friends in attendance. It was admirable that my husband decided to raise another man's child as his own. A few months later, we discussed having another child and I got pregnant almost immediately. We learned that September that we were having another child. I was elated and he seemed happy to be having a child of his own finally. That's when he began to grow distant.

His work environment had major negative influences on him. He primarily worked around single men who had no responsibilities and served their own selfish desires. He tried to be a husband—paying the bills, making sure that we didn't go hungry. That is, until he came home from work one night at three o'clock in the morning and announced that he was moving out.

He moved out that night. No explanation, nothing. Did I mention that I was nine months pregnant with *his* child at the time? I called him when I went into labor. He showed up at the hospital to meet his son;

however, we never lived together again as husband and wife. Having a long marriage like that of my grandparents was my goal; yet that goal—my perfect dream, was screaming that it was all coming to an end...and fast. Well, he left that night. After months of multiple attempts to reconcile while refusing to believe that I had been dumped, he left for good. No explanation. No letter on the pillow...only more heartbreak. I decided to file for divorce and move on. He hasn't seen either of our sons from that day 'til this one.

I could not understand how he could be father to a child who was not his biologically, but leave when it was time to have his own child. This puzzled me for many years. I thought that I had done something wrong—thought that I wasn't a good-enough housekeeper, didn't cook often enough, wasn't sexy enough. Something had to explain his reasoning to leave.

I observed other relationships around me. At the time, my parents had been married over 20 years. My grandparents had been married over 40 years. I was the first person I knew personally to get a divorce. That didn't sit well with me. I was angry. The life I planned was not working out the way it should have.

When he and I spoke after 13 years, he admitted that he simply wasn't ready for that kind of responsibility. I wish that was a conversation he had with me before he decided to bail. My anger turned into bitterness. Bitterness spewed word curses and inner vows that left me trapped and in bondage to my own greatest fears. I was tired of carrying that burden. He sounded remorseful that he had not seen his son since he was a newborn. I sent pictures of both boys so at least he would know what they looked like. At the time of this conversation, we both had remarried, but it was much needed closure for a very old wound.

Dear Angry, Abandoned Wife,

Hebrews 12:15 in the Amplified Bible, Classic Edition (AMPC) reads, "Exercise foresight *and* be on the watch to look [after one another], to see that no one falls back from *and* fails to secure God's grace (His unmerited favor and spiritual blessing), in order that no root of resentment (rancor, bitterness, or hatred) shoots forth and causes trouble *and* bitter torment, and the many become contaminated *and* defiled by it-".

Your situation may not read the same as mine. More than likely, your story has different characters, but similar results. Was it difficult to say their name? Were you reminded of what that person did and became angry all over again, as if it had only happened yesterday? These are the types of things that create a root of resentment. I resented the fact that he left. I resented the fact that he couldn't tell me how he was feeling. I was bitter about his choice to leave me while I was pregnant with his child, as if we meant nothing. My anger and bitterness did not harm him. He continued living his life; I was the one hurting.

I became contaminated and defiled by the thing done to me, just as the Scriptures said. I allowed someone else to have that power over me, my emotions, and my immediate outcomes. I didn't enter into a healthy intimate relationship until a few years later, all as a result of not dealing with this in a healthy way. I clammed up. I built a wall around my heart. I didn't talk about what happened to me. I tried to move forward with life, not knowing I had this huge, exposed wound that was getting more and more infected by the day. It was exposed due to the following labels that I wore: *divorced, single mother,* and *welfare recipient.* It was infected because I had internalized the negative connotations associated with those labels. I needed to learn that my situation does not define me. I needed to take back that power over my emotions. He could not have it any longer. He had taken enough from me.

My release came when I decided to *forgive*. I had to forgive for my own health. I chose to forgive as an act of my will, not because he was innocent. He was wrong and has to make an account for his actions, but I had to learn to trust God—even when I could not trust a man who I accepted as my husband before God and witnesses. I needed to understand that although my husband abandoned me and the children, God never left me. It was me who chose not to lean on Him, but instead leaned to my own understanding.

I encourage you to examine your life. Know that God did not orchestrate your hurt. People don't always listen when God speaks and tells them to turn from their wicked ways and selfish decisions. God made provision in His Word for you to be healed and made whole. As you get to know God through His Word, the healing will come. Be open to how God will lead you to find forgiveness.

Discussion Questions:

1. Which situations left you feeling hurt and abandoned? Write these down.

2. Have you ever felt rejected or unwilling to trust others? Describe what this is like for you.

3. Are you willing to make a choice to forgive—not for their sake, but for your own?

4. If you choose to forgive, here is a prayer that you can recite as often as needed. You may not *feel* like you've forgiven them initially, but this is a process. You did not build up the anger in your heart overnight, so healing may not come overnight. Don't get discouraged. Keep doing your part to get free.

Dear Lord,

Thank you for caring for me enough to want me to heal from this hurt. I release my pain, my hurt, my anger and my resentment to you now by an act of my will. I ask that you create in me a clean heart and renew a right spirit within me (Psalm 51:10). Show me how to live my life free from unforgiveness. I chose to forgive (insert name) and release them to you. I pray that they receive any healing they may need so no one else has to go through pain and suffering. Help me to not give up as You take me through this process, in Jesus' name. Amen.

CHAPTER TWO

MOMMY NEEDS A TIME OUT!

You mean that I can actually drop my kids off and not have to stay with them? I can come back at the end of class and pick them up? These are the thoughts that raced through my head after the instructor clearly said "...bye. See you at 8!"

For the first time since the boys were born, I had free time. I didn't know what to do.

A part of me wanted to return home to take care of the laundry and clean the house with no distractions or interruptions; however, I stood motionless. For the first time in a long time, I realized that I am a woman outside of being a mother. At that moment, I knew with clarity what the next 90 minutes of freedom would entail: a nice, long, hot bubble bath while enjoying my favorite playlist. Blissful pleasure.

After that delightful moment of leisure, I began to seek other experiences for my children to participate in. Extracurricular activities, Vacation Bible School, summer classes and/or programs—you name it, they were there. What I didn't realize at the time was that with having five children, I would be the primary one doing all the transporting. My full schedule bordered on chaos as the years went on. The children got older, each with separate interests, different hobbies, and multiple social events.

The funds to take a vacation did not

exist. Over time, I found myself becoming more resentful, angry even. I love my children, but the daily tasks became overwhelming. I called on my support system whenever I could, but not at the expense of feeling guilty. I prided myself on the fact that the majority of the time, my children were with me. I wasn't the mother always looking for a sitter. I wasn't going out every weekend. I rarely went to the movies, shopping, out with friends, or even celebrated my birthday. As a matter of fact, I barely went out at all. I continued to struggle, day after day, week after week, month after month, year after year—all while growing more upset that no one noticed my sacrifices. I wanted someone to notice and help, but I said nothing.

That seed of resentment did nothing for my personal relationships. Now in my second marriage, I still operated as an independent woman. That inner vow was to never depend on a man again. I did what needed to be done, but it wasn't with a glad heart. I needed him to rescue me, but how can your husband rescue you from *you*?

Well, God must have heard my prayers. With a promotion at work, I was suddenly eligible for company-sponsored travel to various conferences around the country. My very first opportunity was in Clearwater, Florida. I remember checking into the hotel, getting my room key, opening the door, and exhaling. I sat my suitcase down and realized that I was starving. At that moment, the slightest smile stretched across my face. A smile whose presence had long been forgotten, but we were about to become reacquainted. I stretched across the bed, finally understanding that on this trip, I was alone. I didn't have to ask six other people where or what they wanted to eat. I didn't have to cast votes or compromise to make anyone else happy. I could eat where I wanted to for a change. I could come and go as I please, and without a curfew!

It's amazing how as a parent, you

begin to restrict your own activities based on the responsibilities you have to others. That year, I got my time out. I began to enjoy life again...and it felt great!

Dear Angry, Resentful Mom:

Exodus 33:14 NIV reads, "The LORD replied, "My presence will go with you, and I will give you rest." Unfortunately, so many of us fail to recognize that we are no good to anyone else if we do not take care of ourselves. You cannot pour into others from an empty vessel. It is only when we are at our best that we can truly care for others—be it children, a spouse, parents, or other loved ones.

Did my story help you to realize areas where you need to make some adjustments? Whether you choose to take a daily mental health break, take a nice, long bath, or plan a formal vacation to get away—take some time just for you. It's needed. It doesn't have to cost anything, but you are well worth it and your soul will thank you.

Discussion Questions:

1. Have you ever felt like you were just walking through life on auto pilot?

2. At what point did you realize that you needed a break?

3. Did you think it was someone else's responsibility to come to your rescue?

4. What did you do to get that much needed rest?

5. Were you able to recognize that you needed rest before it was too late?

6. How much of the 24 hours we're given do you dedicate to yourself? Make an investment in you through self-care, then write down when and how often.

Dear Heavenly Father,

Thank you for providing for me and my family. I am grateful for the opportunities that you have given us. I thank you in advance for me seeing my own value and making time, whether its five minutes or five hours, to invest in myself. I recognize that I need to be well in order to take care of my family. Help me to prosper and be in health even as my soul prospers (3 John 1:2) in Jesus' name. Amen.

CHAPTER THREE

WHEN SICKNESS SEIZED ME

The more the pressure built, the slower they moved. Filling with fluid, the anticipation of becoming immobile became a credible threat.

While that statement may appear to describe any number of scenarios—a ride at the water park, an animal trying to escape a flood—unfortunately, it refers to my knees. Less than one month away from my 41st birthday, my knees and legs became so swollen that I could barely walk. It was virtually impossible to take the stairs, and it hurt terribly to get in and out of my car. I had no choice but to contact my primary care physician for a same day appointment.

She was so kind with her touch as she felt the fluid buildup around my knees. She wrapped them with Ace bandages and sent me for tests, promising to contact me with the results. I wasn't expecting a phone call on my cell instructing me to go straight to emergency the following day after the lab results came back. I really didn't expect to hear that the hospital was going to admit me. I didn't understand how a few lab tests could cause such reaction.

Suddenly, the focus was not on why I could barely walk. It was on the numbers listed within my lab results. My platelet count had dropped to seven. Normal platelet levels are above 450. Gums bleeding while brushing my teeth could have ended my life. The doctors had to figure out what caused my platelet count to drop so low. The hospital staff came in to explain the number of examinations required of me. At the bottom of the list was a simple ultrasound; however, at the top of the list was a bone biopsy.

I began to panic. Whenever I panic, I break out in hives. So, in addition to a lovely, orange Push-Up ice cream looking goo oozing through the IV to replace my platelets, I got a shot of Benadryl. That liquid Benadryl felt like vodka going through my veins. Suddenly, I wasn't nervous or panicky anymore. Keeping my eyes open to converse with my mom, best friend, pastor, and others who visited me in the hospital became a daunting task. I guess they figured I needed to enjoy that Benadryl-induced sleep because the next thing I remember is waking up to the results of my ultrasound.

They hadn't found the cause of my platelet drop, but they found kidney stones and a small tumor on my liver. Great. Come in for one thing and leave knowing five other things I wished I didn't know. The diagnosis was ITP – idiopathic thrombocytopenic purpura, an autoimmune disorder that destroys the platelets needed for blood clotting. My treatment included six months of a steroid called Prednisone, which causes weight gain.

I no longer recognized myself in the mirror. I was angry about gaining so much weight from the steroids. I was angry that my body wasn't as physically fit as I was used to feeling. I was angry for having to sit in a waiting room with the elderly, who gave me the side eye as if I were too young to need physical therapy. I was angry for having to take so much time off work for the multiple appointments and lab work. The good news is after six months, my platelet count was stable and I was able to walk just fine thanks to therapy. The weight gain is another story. That was a rough year all around.

Dear Angry, Sick, and Tired:

Proverbs 4:20-22 CEV read, "My child, listen carefully to everything I say. Don't forget a single word, but think about it all. Knowing these teachings will mean true life and good health for you." Sickness and illness were things I never worried much about. I took care of others who had been sick, but that wasn't my story.

I didn't look at the elderly or disabled the same after that. I had a new appreciation for accessible buildings and shower facilities after that. This entire experience was an eye-opener. Not only did it open my eyes about my physical health, but it opened my eyes to the true meaning of "by His wounds, you have been healed" (I Peter 2:24 ESV). It is not God's desire for us to experience sickness or disease. If that were the case, He would not have made provision for Jesus to bear the pain so that we would receive healing.

Sickness is not punishment from God. Whatever the diagnosis is, as an heir of God and joint-heir with Christ, claim your healing!

Discussion Questions:

1. Do you know what the Bible says about sickness, illness, and disease? Write at least one Scripture here.

2. Have you ever felt like you were sick because you were being punished for something you did wrong? Does this align with Scripture or contradict it?

3. Do you accept every medical diagnosis without seeking to understand root causes and do you allow that diagnosis to define who you are?

4. Do you even pay attention to how daily activities play a role in your overall health?

Father God,

Help me to claim the victory that is mine according to Your holy Word. Teach me the Scriptures that I can hold onto as your promises. Remind me that Your angels watch over Your Word to perform it (Jeremiah 1:12) so that I am reminded that healing is mine. I thank you for tearing down myths and false teaching about healing that contradict your Scriptures, in Jesus' name. Amen.

CHAPTER FOUR

PEOPLE PLEASING

As the baby in the family, everyone expected me to be docile and accommodating. I sat back and did that for as long as I could; but at some point, as you could probably predict, I had enough. My blood was boiling and finally exploded during a family meeting. With no kind words, I let everyone present—my mom and dad included—know that they would no longer be allowed to tell me what to do or how to do it, and then I stormed out. It was the end for me but also a beautiful beginning. I had shed the expectations of others and could finally get to know me.

Getting to know me was no easy task. I had been a mother and wife for the majority of my adult life. I had to take it slow and tackle the small things first like learning what I like and didn't like to eat. From there, I advanced to what I enjoyed wearing and didn't like wearing. As the youngest child, I had a lifetime of hand-me-downs. Too often, it was based on other people's preferred styles, so I got no vote. I found that I actually enjoyed thrifting and saving money; but this time, I got to choose the styles and colors that I liked. I love one-shoulder outfits; it's my signature style. I also love thigh-high boots which I realized was due to the influence of Rick James.

After clothes came the hardest discovery—what do I enjoy doing with my time. This is where I had to give myself permission to be boring. I'm an introvert who enjoys being at home, reading a good book or watching a video that will help me improve my life. I don't like being around crowds, even if it's family. The quiet life is a definite win for me, so I know I need to plan social activities so I can still recharge in solitude. Learning about myself allowed me to walk away from other's expectations with no guilt. I love it here!

Dear People Pleaser,

Getting over my people pleasing tendencies was not an easy task. It took time, reflection and honesty with myself first. It may also help to practice saying *no*, even if it's only in the mirror every day. It's a muscle that you have to build up so you are okay with saying no without feeling guilty. The word *no* is a complete sentence. Once you learn to say *no*, offering a reason for your response is a courtesy—not a requirement. You do not have to meet other's expectations or explain yourself unless you choose to. Now, go live your best life!

Discussion Questions:

1. When did you realize you were a people pleaser?

2. How does it feel that you've been pleasing everyone else but yourself?

3. What deliberate steps will you take to learn more about your likes and dislikes?

4. Who's the first person you need to practice saying *no* to?

Lord Jesus,

Thank you for bringing this to my attention. I've been focused on pleasing others and ignoring my own needs. Not only have I been ignoring me, but I've been neglecting you. I repent for not honoring you as the Lord of my life. Help me to change my habits and balance my expectations for your glory, in Jesus' name. Amen.

CHAPTER FIVE

WHEN DEATH CAME KNOCKING

"Have you been on Facebook?" the caller asked.

"No," my husband responded.

"You need to check Facebook."

No words can accurately describe the frantic pace at which my husband opened his Facebook account and confirmed his worst nightmare. Not only did he learn that his son and namesake had been tragically murdered, but his ex-wife didn't have the decency to call him and tell him herself. Needless to say, I was angry for him.

The sound that projected from my husband next is one that I will never forget. It was a sharp, piercing "Noooooooo!" that ended only with violent shuddering of his body. All I could do was hold him while he tried his best to grasp this horrifying news.

"I just talked to him," my husband managed to say after he regained some type of composure as he reflected on a conversation he had with his son not 24 hours prior.

It was an icy Saturday night in Michigan that turned a 45-minute drive nearly into a two-hour drive. We arrived at the police station to speak with the homicide detective, who was polite enough to step outside to speak to my husband. His ex-wife was inside the station and they had not seen each other face-to-face in over 15 years.

His daughter informed us of a prayer vigil to be held in Trey's honor on Monday, but later called to say that it had been changed to Tuesday instead. Imagine our surprise to find out that not only was the prayer vigil actually held on Monday, but she intentionally lied at the coaxing of her mother so we would not be present. As a result, I turned my anger into action and took matters into my own hands. Unable to get reliable information directly from the source, I called the morgue to find out the date and time of the viewing. This time, it was the ex-wife who was surprised when she and her husband showed up to find me and my husband waiting to view the body as a family. Even Trey's girlfriend was with them; but you couldn't tell his biological father?

Talk about awkward. A waiting area with ex-spouses, new spouses, children, and a grandchild was filled with niceties as we took turns spending our final moments with

Brian Aldin Matthews III before his body would be cremated. To fathom that she would have cremated his body with no communication with his dad about his death is unbelievable and cruel.

You might be wondering why the animosity on her behalf. Well, their marriage ended when she moved another man into their marital home while her husband still lived there and paid the bills. A decade-long game of cat and mouse ensued as she attempted to keep him out of their children's lives by not sharing their address or the new city they had moved to. Only reconnecting with his children after they turned 18 years old, my husband was finally in a good place with restored relationships and regular communication with them.

As if that tragedy was not enough, my mother had a stroke that same month and was hospitalized for almost two weeks before transferring to a rehabilitation facility. Adding insult to injury, my oldest daughter, a lupus warrior, was hospitalized only four days after Trey's murder. To say that this was a tragic time is a drastic understatement. This all took place in January 2020, a few months shy of the pandemic that impacted the entire globe. During April of 2020, we lost four family members within one week, two of which to COVID-19. Grief had not only come to visit; it became a constant bedfellow.

Dear Grieving and Lonely,

A friend reminded me to be kind to myself, so that is the advice that I offer to you. Healing looks different for different people. No two journeys are alike. My turning point was when I could finally talk about my dad being gone without crying. I can smile now when I share memories of any of the relatives we have lost during this time. I even supported another mom's funeral expenses who recently buried her child. Although you may not have recognized your "corner to turn," it's coming. Just keep pressing forward.

Discussion Questions:

1. Have you ever found out about a loved one's death on social media?

2. If so, were any apologies offered?

3. How has that experience caused you to interact differently yourself?

4. In what ways has grief turned your life upside down?

5. What did you do to "recover"?

Heavenly Father,

Thank you for the comfort of Your Holy Spirit in times of grief and chaos. I appreciate being able to run to You. You are my strong tower where I can run to hide, to vent, to recover and continue being the best I can be. Please help me to forgive others for their mistakes, whether intentional or not, and to not hold grudges. May I continue to love as you have loved me, in Jesus' name. Amen.

CHAPTER SIX

THE SANDWICH GENERATION

Upon leaving rehab, my mother came to stay with me for a couple weeks while my father attempted to have their furnace repaired. When she was able to go home, my father struggled to adjust to the fact that his wife could no longer handle all the tasks that she had previously handled. He tried as best as he could to manage, but it became obvious that he was overwhelmed.

Already struggling with Parkinson's disease, my father's health took a turn for the worse. Drastic weight loss and numerous falls plagued my father's life over the coming months. Visits to the emergency room became the norm.

December 31, 2020 was the last time my mother or my father lived at home on their own. That evening, I received a startling phone call that my dad had fallen. His face was swollen and Mom could not verbalize any helpful information. My sister arrived only moments before I did and we both watched the emergency medical technicians (EMTs) carry a frail version of the muscular man my father once was to the ambulance. He remained hospitalized just shy of one month. From there to rehab. From rehab to a nursing home. From the nursing home to his eternal resting place on June 2, 2021.

That same fateful night, Mom came home to live with me. My days started at 4 a.m., getting up with Mom to get her washed up, dressed and fed before I had to do the same for myself to prepare for work. The evening routine was not much different. She was an early riser who liked to be in bed around 6:30 p.m., This only meant me having to rush home from work to feed her before she got sleepy.

Mom tried to escape multiple times. She succeeded once, only to be picked up by the local police—wearing a pair of footed pajamas in the snow. Unable to tell her name or address, they were kind enough to take her to the hospital where it was finally confirmed that she had vascular dementia. I started a new job just five days after she came to live with me and she needed 24-hour care. I depended on family members to sit with her during the day while the rest of the household went to work and school. We juggled our schedules for four months when I made the difficult decision to move her to memory care.

My life had been turned upside down in a short amount of time. I had my first medical procedure where my mother was not by my side. When I got sick in the past, I would climb in my mother's comfy king-sized bed and be nursed back to health. I could no longer call and hear her voice, as she was mostly non-verbal. No more watching Westerns on television with my dad, shopping for cars together or even celebrating their newest great-grand child. I couldn't even bring myself to send the thank you cards to acknowledge the many acts of kindness shown during my dad's death. My new life was beginning without a father while being the primary caregiver for my mother and being a parent to my own children.

As the days continued with caring for my mom, I realized that I had become a part of "the sandwich generation." This term is used to describe those who have and may still be caring for their children while caring for their elderly or aging parents. As we are enjoying our adult years, we often forget that our parents are getting older, too. Within a few years, my parents went from being strong and independent to becoming frail and helpless. I cared for them both as they experienced their final days in the earth realm.

It was hard explaining to my dad why no one was coming to visit him in the nursing home. I reassured him that no, it wasn't because we didn't love him. It was hard explaining a global pandemic to two people who had been able to freely come and go as they pleased. It was difficult getting them to keep a mask on that was both uncomfortable and viewed as unnecessary with impaired cognitive processing. Securing the necessary documents to verify insurance coverage, the constant faxing and emailing the durable power of attorney document and other endless tasks were daunting. Trying to care for my own home while maintaining their family home with its utility bills and needed repairs was tantamount to running around like a chicken with its head cut off.

As if the caretaking wasn't bad enough, the fact that I had to manage the financial burden of mom's care *alone* was even more heartbreaking. It was the best choice for mom to move into memory care. I researched multiple facilities to find one that I could trust. I considered multiple options before deciding that the financial sacrifice would be hard, hoping that my sister or others would at least contribute something. In the end, I depleted my savings, cashed in their stocks and bonds and sold their home to be able to give her 24/7 care until her final day, January 18, 2023.

I believe making necessary preparations in advance. When I was 21 years old, I asked my mother to write her obituary. If she did write her own obituary, I never found it; however, Mom did have the forethought to secure a mausoleum for herself and my dad. That made the transition easier. Although I had anticipated her death since my dad passed, it did not make the finality of it any easier.

Dear Strong One,

I know you're tired of going through it, but you're going to get through it. Make sure you are keeping your cup filled; otherwise, you will not be able to pour into anyone else. Remember to pour from your overflow and not your cup. The cup is for you; the overflow is for everyone else. It is easy to be angry that the majority of the responsibility falls on you when there are others who can help. In the final analysis, take comfort that you did what was needed to be done for your loved one(s). There may not be much time between your caretaking responsibilities, but a few moments of reflection, connection, enjoying nature and even eating your favorite meal does so much for your own wellbeing. Take care of yourself in the process.

Discussion Questions:

1. Have you had the responsibility of caring for or funding a loved one's care?

2. Did others offer to assist or were you left to handle it on your own?

3. How did you feel during that experience?

4. If it has ended, how do you feel looking back on this time?

5. What advice would you offer others who find themselves in this space?

Holy Spirit,

Is there anything that I'm carrying that would cause me to not represent you well today? May You grant me the power to be strengthened in my innermost being so that Christ Jesus can dwell in my heart through faith, and that I may remain rooted and grounded in love (Ephesians 3:16-17), not anger. Thank you for the peace of God which surpasses all understanding to soothe my heart and mind through Christ Jesus (Philippians 4:7), my Lord and Savior, in Jesus' name. Amen.

CHAPTER SEVEN

SUPPRESSED OR HEALED?

Anger has a way of being masked by other emotions. Most people knew me as this nice, sweet "good" girl. I'd be sweet, courteous, kind and easy to get along with; but as soon as you made me mad, I'd blow up and say all the stuff I had been storing up while acting "sweet." That's not healthy. We should be able to say what's on our minds without pacifying our feelings for the benefit of others.

It's often hard to discover if you are really healed from rage until you're placed in a situation that triggers you. In those moments, you may blow up, which indicates that your anger was only suppressed. It was not truly gone; it was dormant or waiting for the right moment to rear its ugly head.

I never really understood that I was holding on to the notion of protecting myself so tightly, until I realized that I was too fearful to let anything else into my life. You see, when you're holding onto one thing, your hand simply cannot grasp something else. You first have to let go of that thing that you've been holding onto out of fear of letting it go. For me, it was my past.

"Hello, my name is De'Andrea, and I am a recovering perfectionist." Oh, yeah, I can say it and laugh now; however, I remember a time not that long ago when the mere thought of being transparent scared the crap out of me.

What does being a perfectionist have to do with my past? Well, I wanted my life to be perfect. I had never envisioned it any other way. (Does anybody?) Things were going pretty well. I had graduated from high school as number 11 in a class of over 600. I was the "good girl" who could do no wrong...or so "they" thought. See, the thing with setting such high expectations is #1: they're not realistic, and #2: it's impossible to maintain. Sure, I went away to college and continued to excel. That is, until I got pregnant.

The crazy thing about religion is you do what you're told (most of the time) without understanding why you're being asked to do (or not do) those things. I had not "grown up in the church," but my family did attend regularly. We attended on the second and fourth Sundays of the month. It wasn't until I went down south for a summer vacation that I understood why. The country preacher was only at the church in their town on the second and fourth Sundays. On the first and third Sundays, he was preaching at the church in the next town, so they had those weeks off.

From age eleven until sixteen, I was exposed to religion, the very formal teachings of the Bible, God and Jesus. It was never personal. There was no talk of having a relationship with God. There was no mention of the Holy Spirit, although I knew something made those folks pop up like popcorn when the singing was real good.

It is not a sign of weakness to ask for help. I've been influenced by a family of "do-it-yourselfers." As a child, I saw that there was no project too big or small for my grandaddy. I never recall the roof leaking, but he was up on the roof fixing it one summer with me holding the ladder. The porch encasement looked fine to me, but there we were tearing out the bricks and mixing the concrete to fill them back in straight and new. From these experiences, I was taught that there was nothing beyond the capabilities of a little "elbow grease." Whatever needed to be done, you somehow figured out on your own how to do it.

The part that I could not see at the time was Daddy only had experience in the area that he worked. He did construction, so he was skilled at those trades, but he was not perfect and did not know everything. All I knew about his work was the treat that he'd save me from his lunch pail. The lunch pail itself is another fond memory. When his car would pull into the driveway, I'd run to the window with my sister to make sure it was him. Then, we'd greet him with a big hug. There I stood, eye to eye with a black aluminum lunch pail. I wasn't quite tall enough to look eye-to-eye with anything else, so we had a special relationship, although short-lived.

Inside the sturdy container was a pleasant surprise for a girl who tried her best to be good that day. I couldn't complain when Daddy was no longer working, no longer pulling in the driveway, lunch pail in hand. I had him all day and that was better than the sweet treats after a long day of "trying" to be good.

I often tried real hard in my adult life to do the things that I thought I ought to do. After much hurt and disappointment, I got tired of trying. I had been hurt, but could not show it. I had to be strong for my boys. That tough outer exterior began to resemble that aluminum lunch pail, only I didn't know who the fortunate lad would be who unlocked its sweet treasure.

It was a hot day in August when that do-it-yourself attitude had me in the driveway removing lug nuts while changing my own flat tire. After removing four lugs with no problem, the fifth one wouldn't budge. I had no choice but to accept defeat and drive ever so slowly to the nearest full-service station. (Yes, they were still around). Well, that's where I met my second husband.

I had a terrible habit of threatening

divorce every time I got upset with my husband. To be honest, I was actually afraid that he would leave...like my first husband did. To threaten divorce was my defense mechanism, to "beat him to the punch." Learning to cope with conflict in a relationship was new to me. Fighting, I was accustomed to. Throwing things, I was accustomed to. "Bitching," I was accustomed to. Working on a long-term marital strategy, I was *not* accustomed to.

Through it all, he learned how to deal with me before I could get me under control. He often diffused a situation with humor, much to my dismay. Humor is not something I embrace, but it was essential for keeping the tension low in our relationship. It helped the thunder and lightning of the storm to pass so that clear skies can return. Our "togetherness" had changed, and I'm not sure if it was for the better. Jobs, children and responsibilities have changed the landscape of our marriage many times.

Looking back, I, or my sense of self was lost somewhere in the process. You never know how strong a relationship is until it's tested.

Discussion Questions:

1. Did you ever suppress your emotions? If so, what was the result?

2. How did you deal with it when your childhood coping mechanisms threatened your relationship(s)?

3. Were you able to maintain or did you move on?

4. Are you healed or are you still pursuing your healing?

5. What methods have been helpful for you?

All Knowing God,

You know the beginning from the end. You knew me before I was in my mother's womb. I thank You that You can turn everything I've experienced around for my good. Some decisions that I've made have not been the best and probably did not align with Your will. I repent and want to learn to trust You more. Please lead me and guide me so I don't depend on myself, but come to depend on you, my Lord and my King, in Jesus' name. Amen.

EPILOGUE

With each symptom, sign or change, there is a root cause, personal history and an open door that allowed the spirit of anger to enter. Once you recognize the spirit of anger by diagnosing the symptoms, you must get to the root cause of when it started. This will let you know if there was something in your personal history that initiated the spirit of anger or if it is generational, which means it began in your bloodline long before your birth. In the following timeline, you will see the impact of generational anger through the life of Moses. In the final analysis, you should repent for your behavior and that of your ancestors if it's generational. You should renounce association with prior anger triggers, change your habits/responses and discipline your tongue. These steps can help you get back to God's original intent for your life.

- Open Door – Moses carried the spirit of rejection
  - o Rejected by mom due to Pharoah's orders to kill boys under age two
  - o Rejected by the Hebrews for growing up in the palace
  - o Rejected by Pharoah when Moses returned representing God
  - o Rejected by Miriam and Aaron when they said the Lord doesn't only speak to you (**Numbers 12:1-2**)
- Personal History – Rejection gave way to anger
  - o **Exodus 2:11-12** – an Egyptian hit a Hebrew; Moses got angry

and his anger (rage) led to murder.

- o **Exodus 11:8** – Moses left Pharoah in great anger after Pharoah didn't keep his word to let the people go.
- o **Exodus 32:15-19** – The Ten Commandments, the golden calf; Moses' anger waxed hot.
- o **Numbers 20:10-13** – He struck the rock twice instead of speaking to it like the Lord said; told he would not enter the Promised Land.

- Root cause – A generational word curse that had not been broken
  - o **Exodus 6:16-20**
    - Jacob was the father of Levi.
    - Levi was the father of Gershom, Kohath and Merari.
    - Kohath was the father of Amram.

- Amram was the father of Aaron, Moses and Miriam (4th generation).
- **Genesis 49:1-2,5-7**
  - Simeon and Levi; weapons of violence; Israel (Jacob) was not in agreement with what was done; cursed for their fierce anger and cruel wrath.
  - Be careful what you speak over your children; it can alter their destiny.
- **Genesis 34:1-4; 8-22**
  - The rape of Dinah (daughter of Leah and Jacob) by Shechem the Hivite; he fell in love with her after the rape and asked for her hand in marriage.
  - Levi and Simeon sought revenge; planned to have the men circumcised in

- order for Dinah to marry Shechem.
- While they were still sore (day three), Simeon and Levi killed all the males, took their herds, houses, wives and children.
- God changed Jacob's name to Israel right after this. Although he had changed, his trickster ways were passed down to his children.
- Jacob never addressed what was did, although he talked to them about it until his deathbed.

- God's Original Intent – **Numbers 12:3**
  - Moses was a meek and faithful man. Although anointed and had accomplished great things, he did not fulfill his divine purpose to lead the Israelites into the Promised Land of Canaan.

- o We must enforce the verdict made on the cross.
- o Every curse you don't deal with deals with you.

As we look at the life of Moses, hopefully you recognize and pay attention to the patterns so you can diagnose the root cause in your own life. It's time to shut the open doors that gave the enemy legal access to oppress you through anger all these years. My prayer for you is to learn God's original intent and to align with His will so you can accomplish all that you were created to do!

As we close this chapter on anger, here is a daily affirmation as you continue your journey of mastering anger:

Today, I declare that anger no longer controls me.

I have developed self-control and align with God's plan for my life.

I release all unforgiveness, resentment and bitterness. Every void is filled. I am healed and whole!

<u>Non-Fiction Titles by Dr. De'Andrea Matthews</u>

The Overcomers' Anthology: Volume One

The Overcomers' Anthology: Volume Two – Overcoming Fear

31-Day Devotional for Lupus Warriors

The Published Professional:
Writing a Book to Build Your Brand (eBook
only)

The Power of Prayer: An Anthology

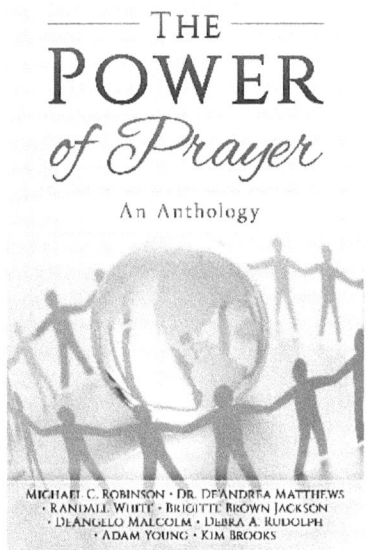

If you have read any of these books, don't forget to leave a review!

Other compilations featuring book chapters from
Dr. De'Andrea Matthews

Insights: The Proven Strategies for Success –
How Entrepreneurs Thrive in the Modern
World and How You Can Too
by Antoine Airoldi

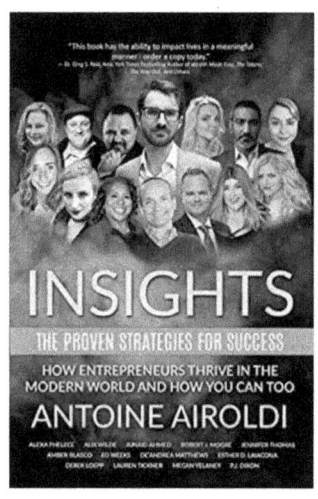

Campus Diversity Triumphs: Valleys of Hope
(Diversity in Higher Education) by Dr.
Sherwood Thompson

Exploring Campus Diversity: Case Studies and Exercises by Dr. Sherwood Thompson

Magnetic Entrepreneur:
My Success Formula by Robert J. Moore

ABOUT THE AUTHOR

Committed to edifying the kingdom of God, Dr. De'Andrea Matthews serves as senior pastor of Visions International Ministry where she teaches, trains and activates leaders to heal from trauma, experience victory over darkness and walk in their divine destinies. An international speaker and award-winning author, Dr. Matthews turned adversity into her advantage by showing others how to triumph over tragedy to become their greatest possible selves. Graced with an abundance of gifts and over 25 years of ministry experience, Dr. Matthews is paving the way for many to grow and thrive spiritually and professionally.

www.ingramcontent.com/pod-product-compliance
Lightning Source LLC
Chambersburg PA
CBHW051547120626
46551CB00013B/1404